ALL

Sandra Woodcock

Published in association with The Basic Skills Agency

Hodder & Stoughton

A MEMBER OF THE HODDER HEADLINE GROUP

Acknowledgements
Cover: Jonathon Daniel/Allsport.
Photos: pp. 3, 16, 25 © Action-Plus Photographic; pp. 19, 23 Corbis; p. 21 © Pacha/Corbis; p. 6 Allsport USA.

Orders: please contact Bookpoint Ltd, 39 Milton Park, Abingdon, Oxon OX14 4TD. Telephone: (44) 01235 400414, Fax: (44) 01235 400454. Lines are open from 9.00–6.00, Monday to Saturday, with a 24 hour message answering service. Email address: orders@bookpoint.co.uk

British Library Cataloguing in Publication Data
A catalogue record for this title is available from The British Library

ISBN 0 340 74712 9

First published 1999
Impression number 10 9 8 7 6 5 4 3 2 1
Year   2004 2003 2002 2001 2000 1999

Copyright © 1999 Sandra Woodcock

Typeset by Fakenham Photosetting Ltd, Fakenham, Norfolk.
Printed in Great Britain for Hodder & Stoughton Educational, a division of Hodder Headline Plc, 338 Euston Road, London NW1 3BH by Redwood Books, Trowbridge, Wiltshire.

Contents

1   The Scene

Nick is visiting his cousin Ed,
who lives in America.
He has been there for just three days
but already he's missing football.
Ed is going to take him to a basketball game.
Nick doesn't know much about the game
but he has seen it on the TV.

2   The Game Explained

Ed   You don't look too keen
         on this game, Nick.
         Don't you want to go?

Nick   It's just that I don't know
         much about it.

Ed   Don't worry.
         You'll soon pick it up.
         It's a great game.

Nick   I can tell that from seeing
         some of it on TV last night.
         It seems very exciting.

Ed   That's right.
         It's a very fast game –
         non-stop action.

Nick   Why is it so fast?

A basketball game in action.

Ed   It's because of the clock.
The players are not only trying
to beat the other team,
they have to beat the clock as well.

The aim is to score points
by getting the ball
into the other team's basket.
But it's not that easy.
The rules say that when a team
gets the ball, they have to
make a shot on the basket
within 24 seconds.
If they don't, the other team
gets the ball.

Nick   I saw the clock on the court.
It was huge.

Ed	After someone has scored,
	the other team has to start up again
	in five seconds.
	They have to get the ball
	past the centre line in ten seconds.
Nick	So the pressure is really on them.
	That's why it's so exciting.
Ed	They play in such a small area as well.
	The basketball court is
	28.7m long and 15.2m wide
	so the fans can see and hear
	all the action from close up –
	much better than a football match!
Nick	The players seem to be
	all over the place.
	I can't tell what's going on.

Basketball fans sit close to the game.

Ed	Each team has ten players but only five from each team can be on court at any one time. The others are subs. They swop in and out to keep up the pace of the game. The coach decides when to send in a sub. The players don't have fixed positions. So you will see them all move all over the court.
Nick	So can any of them try to score?
Ed	Yes. Some players play better in defence or as shooters. The best players, though, are good at all the skills of the game – defence, passing and shooting. There are two forwards who play near to the basket, a centre and two guards who play back. Guards shoot from a long range.
Nick	That's why they are all giants!

Ed	The guards are usually the smaller players, but in basketball most players are very tall. The average height of professional players is over 2m.
Nick	That's six foot seven! Who's the tallest player?
Ed	Centres are usually the tallest. I guess Abdul-Jabber must be 2.67m (7ft 2ins). Then there's one player, Bogues, who is only 1.6m (5ft 3ins).
Nick	How many points does the team get when they score?

Ed   That depends on where the player is
when he shoots.
It can be one, two or three points.
There are different zones
shown by lines on the court.
Points depend on
which zone you're in
when you make the shot.

Nick   There don't seem to be many rules
in the game.

Ed   There's a lot of rules.
I told you some of the time rules
but there are others.
Basketball is a non-contact sport.

Nick   No pushing, shoving
or holding another player.

Ed   Right.
No touching another player at all.
Even bumping into a player
can be called a foul.

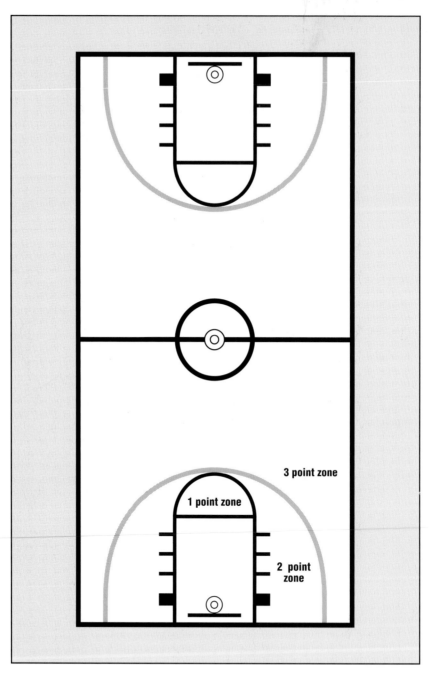

A basketball court.

Nick	That's an impossible rule with such a fast game and no fixed positions!
Ed	That's where the skill comes in. The referees know that some bumps are accidents. They won't always call a foul. But it is an important rule. Any player who commits six personal fouls is sent off.
Nick	Is it true that a player can't run with the ball?
Ed	That's right. No running or walking with the ball. To move it along, they have to dribble. That is bouncing it, with one hand only. As soon as you hold the ball, the dribble is over and you have to pass it.

Nick	You mean you can't start dribbling again once you've stopped?
Ed	That's right. We've been working on dribbling in our school team. It's really hard. You have to dribble without looking at the ball.
Nick	Why?
Ed	Well, you should have your eyes on the basket. That's what you are aiming for. Also, you should be looking all over the court, spotting the gaps, looking for chances to pass. 'Get your head up!' is what the coach keeps telling me.

Nick   I suppose you can kick the ball?

Ed   No way!
You can't punch it with your fist either.
You can only use your hands.

Nick   What happens when players
break the rules?

Ed   It's called a foul.
Contact with another player
is a personal foul.
If there is a foul, the other team
gets a throw in from the sideline.
If the foul was done
while a player is shooting
the other team gets
up to three free throws at the basket.

Nick   Like penalties in football?

Ed   Yes, a nice easy chance to score.
Bad news if you miss!

Nick   What sort of score
do the best players get?

Ed   Well, the record is held
by Will Chamberlain,
who scored 100 points in a single game
in 1962.
He also averaged
50 points a game in that season.
That's a record.
The top point scorer at the moment
is Michael Jordan.
His average is 31 points.

Nick	I've heard of him.
Ed	I bet you have.
	He's the best player of all time.
	That's what I think anyway.
	You should see him dunk!
Nick	What does that mean?
Ed	Dunking? That's a way of shooting.
	It's when a player jumps so high
	he's right above the basket
	and can push the ball in from above.
	It looks really good.
	Players like Jordan
	look as if they're flying!
	The fans love it.
Nick	What is the basketball
	competition called?

Basketball players jump very high.

Ed   Well, in the USA basketball is mainly run
by the NBA. That stands for
National Basketball Association.
There are 29 teams in the NBA.
The season starts in November
and runs through to March.
There are matches every weekend
and all through the week.
In October each team
has a training camp.
They sort out who is going to play
for the season.
It's a chance to see the 'rookies' –
that's first-year players.
The coaches can see
who looks promising.
In February there's the All Star Game
when the best players compete.
It's just for fun.
Then, at the end of the season,
16 teams qualify for play-offs.
In the end two teams get to the final
and the winners are NBA champions
for that season.

Nick	So which teams are the best in America?
Ed	Well, just now it's Chicago Bulls. But Detroit Pistons, Houston Rockets and Los Angeles Lakers are all good. They all have their star players. Boston Celtics have won the NBA the most times.
Nick	This game we are going to is just a college game, isn't it?
Ed	Yes, but that doesn't mean it will be dull. College teams are really the training ground for most of our professional players. You could get to see a top game. You might see the next Michael Jordan or Shaquille O'Neal!

The team badge of the Chicago Bulls.

Nick   Can college boys really get a chance
to go professional so soon?

Ed   They sure can.
A lot of the players quit college
before finishing their education.
The league doesn't want to encourage this,
so they put a limit on what a rookie can earn.
But the long-term prospects are so good
they could soon be earning millions.
Michael Jordan's contract this season
was for 30 million dollars.
Then he gets another 41 million
from use of his name.

Nick   So basketball got him
some good business deals?

Ed   That's right. Lots of the top players
make the most of their fame.
Shaq O'Neal has done rap albums,
films and even stars in a video game.

Michael Jordan in *Space Jam*.

Nick   Why don't we see much basketball
in other countries?

Ed   It's there.
It just doesn't get covered
by the sports news.
Basketball is getting more popular
in lots of countries now.
It got a big boost after people saw
the USA's Dream Team win the gold medal
in the 1992 Olympic Games.
In England you have
the Sheffield Sharks and London Tigers.
In Australia, you have the Perth Wild Cats.
Basketball is also played all over Europe and Asia.

Nick   Well, I don't know of any.
I can't see it taking off back home.
Not like here.

Members of the Dream Team, 1992.

Ed   You never know.
The great thing about the game
is that you don't need much to start off.
You don't have to buy a lot of expensive gear.
Kids play anywhere,
any bit of waste ground,
every school playground.
Wait until you've seen the game.
You could be going home all fired up
and ready to start playing!

Nick   I'm not giving up football yet!
But at least I know more
about basketball now.
I'll be watching very closely tomorrow.

Kids playing basketball in a car park.